Perspectives
Archaeological Treasures
Who Owns Them?

Series Consultant: Linda Hoyt

Flying Start
to Literacy®

Contents

Who owns the past?

Many people who are interested in archaeology believe that artifacts that have been removed from their country of origin for whatever reason should be returned. But there is no simple solution. There are many sides to what has become a serious argument between some countries.

Were these treasures stolen? Or were they saved from being neglected or destroyed? And should they be returned to their original owners?

You decide: who does own the past?

No one owns the past

Max Curtain is a 16-year-old high school student who studies archaeology. He argues that the objects found by archaeologists must be preserved and they must be available to the whole world. Do you agree with Max or not? What is the most convincing part of his argument?

Imagine if you found an old, rusty car in your neighbours' garage, and they said you could take it if you wanted it because it was their great-grandma's and they don't care about it or even want it.

You take the car and clean it up. You give it a new paint job and fix up the engine. Then your neighbours see how nice the car is now and ask for it back. They now realise that their great-grandma actually meant a lot to them and they think the car belongs in the family.

This is how I view countries that have not been organised enough to take care of their archaeological past and suddenly, after treasures have been maintained and preserved in museums, they want them back.

No one owns the past. It doesn't matter if the archaeological discoveries, which could include human remains, structural remains or artifacts, are significant for the original culture and its beliefs. We can't let that limit the analysis and preservation of the material culture. Material culture must be preserved because it is the physical objects and resources that can be used to define a culture. It is very important to keep these objects safe. Although many cultures do treasure the significant artifacts of their ancestors, material culture is important for everyone to learn from.

Archaeology has led to great knowledge and understanding of the past. For example, evidence that human evolution originated in Africa was discovered at the Olduvai Gorge archaeological site in Tanzania, Eastern Africa by Louis and Mary Leakey in the 1930s. This ground-breaking information would never have progressed our understanding of human evolution if people had restricted the excavation because they believed that their ancestors' remains and the area must be left untouched.

An archaeologist brushes sand away from a ceramic artifact.

Archaeologists reveal an ancient hidden floor in Libya.

Another example is the debate between Native Americans and archaeologists in the United States about the *Native American Graves Protection and Repatriation Act* (NAGPRA), which provides for the return of Native American artifacts to the original owners. In 1991, a group of Native Americans signed an agreement with the West Virginia Department of Transportation about the construction of a road near a 2000-year-old burial mound of the Adena people, a pre-Columbian Native American culture. The agreement stated that everything excavated in advance of the road construction near the burial mound had to be handed back to be reburied within a year. This agreement restricted archaeologists from doing an in-depth analysis of the artifacts found. It also prevented any significant artifacts from being displayed in a museum for the public to appreciate and learn from.

If every person who had some relationship to an archaeological find had power over what happened to it, archaeology would never have progressed. The past would still be a mystery. This is why I believe that no matter the circumstances, no one owns the past.

Should the Elgin Marbles be returned to Greece?

Ruth Quinn is a 14-year-old high school student. In this article, she argues that the Elgin Marbles, currently displayed at the British Museum in London, should be returned to Greece.

What do you think? Are you convinced by Ruth's argument?

The sculptures were originally displayed at the Parthenon in Athens, Greece.

The Elgin Marbles, also known as the Parthenon Marbles, are a collection of 2300-year-old marble sculptures moved from Greece to Britain between 1801 and 1812. They are called the Elgin Marbles because it was Lord Elgin, the British ambassador, who decided to ship some of them from the Parthenon in Athens to supposedly protect them from the violence going on between the Turks and the Greeks at that time. He said that he had permission from the Turks. Eventually, the British government purchased the sculptures and displayed them to the public in the British Museum.

From the British point of view, the sculptures were taken to the British Museum to showcase and preserve ancient culture. From the Greek point of view, the sculptures were stolen and the display at the Parthenon was ruined.

Soon after the sculptures were taken, people in Greece started to argue for their return to Athens. They did not think that the Turks had any right to give Elgin the authority to remove the Elgin Marbles. The Greeks have been arguing the same case for 150 years. In my opinion, they should definitely have the sculptures back.

The Elgin Marbles on display in the British Museum

The remaining sculptures have been moved from the Parthenon for safekeeping and restoration in the Acropolis Museum in Athens. Why shouldn't the Elgin Marbles be returned to complete the museum's display? Wouldn't it be more enjoyable for everyone, Greeks and tourists included, if the head of an ancient goddess was returned to her body, or if a sculpted procession was not incomplete?

Imagine if people went to France, took away the Eiffel Tower and displayed it in some other country. Of course, we would think that was totally outrageous. Why doesn't Greece deserve the same respect for their claim to have the Elgin Marbles returned?

There is one important argument put forward against returning the Elgin Marbles. If these ancient artifacts were sent back to their homeland, it could mean many other archaeological treasures would have to be returned to their original owners. This would put all of the world's museums in jeopardy and create a very controversial situation.

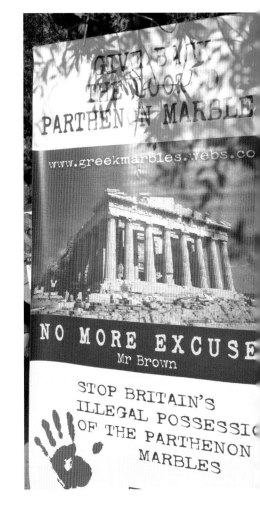

The problem may have originally stemmed from the actual rights of the Greeks as the owners of the sculptures, but now it seems to be something more than that. It seems more about the pride of the two nations in this battle and about who will come out on top.

In my opinion, giving the sculptures back to their original owners is far more important than any other consideration.

Who gets the sunken treasure?

Gold coins and emeralds are obviously valuable treasure. Yet even everyday items become vastly valuable when they acquire historical significance.

In this article, journalist Kathiann Kowalski asks who gets the treasure from underwater shipwrecks – archaeologists, governments, treasure hunters or someone else?

Should shipwrecks be protected by a treaty or be the property of those who find them?

Who owns the *Titanic*?

In 1912, the ship the *Titanic* hit an iceberg and sank to the bottom of
the Atlantic Ocean. Today, the wreck of the *Titanic* is still there. The
problem is that it is in international waters, which are open to the
world at large. They don't belong to anyone. So, who owns the *Titanic*?

A federal court in Virginia in the United States has awarded the
private company RMS Titanic, Inc., exclusive rights to conduct
salvage operations on the 20th-century's most newsworthy shipwreck.

While a court cannot police waters around the wreck, its ruling can
still establish that a company is first on the scene of a particular
shipwreck. Then others within the court's jurisdiction or area of
authority must not interfere with the first company's salvage efforts.
To stop people from countries outside the United States from getting
to the treasure, salvors can ask the courts of other countries to
recognise the first court's ruling.

Beyond ordinary salvage rights, the federal court gave RMS Titanic, Inc., ownership of everything on the *Titanic* – a controversial move.

Companies such as RMS Titanic, Inc., are willing to invest lots of money in the hope of finding sunken treasure. "On the other side, there's government and international concern over what happens to these wrecks from a historical and cultural perspective," says law professor Thomas Schoenbaum at the University of Georgia, in the United States. In other words, the worldwide archaeological community feels there is a public interest in preserving historical riches for everyone.

The *Titanic*, which sank on 15 April, 1912.

Above and right: Artifacts recovered from the wreck of the *Titanic*.

What about history?

A treaty has been proposed by UNESCO, the United Nations Educational, Scientific and Cultural Organization. If approved by enough countries, the treaty will protect many underwater wrecks from salvage. Even with a treaty, disputes may still arise about how individual shipwrecks should be preserved.

The method preferred by archaeologists is to preserve sites in the place where they are found. This approach, such as an underwater archaeological park, would preserve sites for future generations. On the other hand, systematic excavation of parts of some sites could yield valuable information, if they are excavated according to archaeological principles.

How will the issues ultimately be resolved? Like many undiscovered shipwrecks, some answers are still mysteries of the deep.

Look what they found!

In this article, Diana Childress writes about what happened when venues for the 2008 Olympics were constructed across the city of Beijing, China. Without the huge amount of construction for the Olympics, the city's artifacts would have remained undiscovered. Should these artifacts have been left where they were found? What do you think?

Digging down into the earth is like time travel. The subsoil of cities that have existed for hundreds or thousands of years is rich in artifacts, bones and fossils, all clues to life in earlier times.

Fortunately, many countries require that archaeologists who are trained to date and interpret these clues examine construction sites so that cultural relics can be preserved and studied. Like pirates looking for treasure, archaeologists consult old maps to determine where to probe.

The area around Beijing has been the political centre of the country, a magnet for arts, culture and business, and a major transport centre. Human fossils discovered in the 1920s reveal that people lived there as early as 230,000 years ago. The area remained populated through prehistoric times, becoming a strong, walled city-state in the 11th century BCE and later an important regional capital. With all the rich layers of history buried beneath the modern city, builders had to be attentive to what they dug up.

Construction work at the main stadium for the Beijing Olympic Games in 2008.

A 500-year-old temple near the main stadium

The organisers of the Olympics decided to build or renovate 31 sporting venues. Construction supervisors and archaeologists worked together for four years as the grounds were excavated.

In addition to the excavations, archaeologists restored three ancient temples located near Olympic stadiums. One was close to the aquatics centre, where American swimmer Michael Phelps set a record for the number of gold medals won at the Olympics.

In late 2007, the Chinese press summed up the finds: 1538 artifacts of gold, jade, porcelain and other materials; more than 6000 ancient coins; and 700 ancient tombs. The oldest objects found were terracotta pots that date back 2000 years.

A goose-shaped terracotta pot from the Han Dynasty

The richest treasures were located in the hills of western Beijing. From 1368 to 1912, the area had been filled with parks and temples. Wealthy officials of the imperial government supported these temples and often chose to be buried there. An ornate jade belt and elegant bronze urns were among the valuable relics unearthed in mausoleums at the site.

To celebrate China's archaeological wealth, the start of the final relay of the Olympic torch run was staged at the site where "Peking Man", the earliest specimen of *Homo erectus*, had been found in the 1920s.

On completing his relay, Feng Gong, the first torchbearer, expressed his awe: "Though I just ran for 70 to 80 metres, it seemed to me that I had passed through a tunnel of time and space. From primitive stone tools used by prehistoric humans to the Bird's Nest and the Water Cube, human civilisations have been passed down generations to generations, just like the Olympic torch relay."

A reconstruction of Peking Man (inset) and the site where the specimen was discovered.

What is your opinion?: How to write a persuasive argument

1. State your opinion

Think about the issues related to your topic. What is your opinion?

2. Research

Research the information you need to support your opinion.

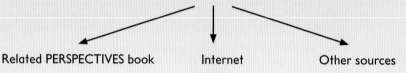

Related PERSPECTIVES book   Internet   Other sources

3. Make a plan

Introduction

How will you "hook" the reader?

State your opinion.

List reasons to support your opinion.

What persuasive devices will you use?

Reason 1
Support your reason with evidence and details.

Reason 2
Support your reason with evidence and details.

Reason 3
Support your reason with evidence and details.

Conclusion

Restate your opinion. Leave your reader with a strong message.

4. Publish

Publish your persuasive argument.

Use visuals to reinforce your opinion.